Natural and Man-made

Revised and Updated

Angela Royston

© 2003, 2008 Heinemann Library
a division of Pearson Inc.
Chicago, Illinois

Customer Service 888-454-2279
Visit our website at www.heinemannraintree.com

Designed by Joanna Hinton-Malivoire
Printed and bound in China by South China Printing Co. Ltd

12 11 10 09 08
10 9 8 7 6 5 4 3 2 1

New edition ISBN-13:   978-1-4329-1448-6 (hardcover)
                         978-1-4329-1470-7 (paperback)
           ISBN-10:   1-4329-1448-0 (hardcover)
                         1-4329-1470-7 (paperback)

The Library of Congress has cataloged the first edition as follows:
Royston, Angela
 Natural and man-made / Angela Royston
   p. cm. – (My World of Science)
 Summary: Provides a simple explaination of the differences between natural
 and man-made materials, including examples of their uses in nature and everyday life.
  Includes bibliographical references and index.
  ISBN 1-40340-856-4 (HC), 1-40343-169-8 (Pbk)
  1. Materials--Juvenile literature.   [1. Materials.] I. Title.
 II. Series: Royston, Angela. My world of science.
 TA403.2.R695 2003
 620.1'1--dc21
                     2002009435

Acknowledgements
The publishers would like to thank the following for permission to reproduce photographs: © Alamy pp. **16** (Frances Roberts), **17** (Westend61); © Corbis pp. **10**, **29** (Saba/J. A. Girodano); © Eye Ubiquitous p. **4** (Julia Bayne); Getty Images p. **25**; Harcourt Education Ltd p. **15** (Tudor Photography); Peter Gould p. **8** inset; Photodisc p. **20**; Rupert Horrox pp. **9**, **14**; Still Pictures p. **8**; Trevor Clifford pp. **5**, **6**, **7**, **11**, **12**, **13**, **18**, **19**, **21**, **22**, **23**, **24**, **26**, **28**; Trip p. **27** (D. Rayers).

Cover photographs reproduced with permission of © Getty Images (CSA Plastock) and © Getty Images (PhotoDisc).

The publishers would like to thank Jon Bliss for his assistance in the preparation of this book.

Every effort has been made to contact copyright holders of any material reproduced in this book. Any omissions will be rectified in subsequent printings if notice is given to the publishers.

Contents

What Is a Natural Material? 4

Some Natural Materials 6

What Is a Man-made Material? 8

Plastic 10

Some Man-made Materials 12

Glass or Plastic? 14

China or Plastic? 16

Wood, Stone, or Plastic? 18

Wax or Plastic? 20

A Mixture of Materials 22

Clothes 24

Warm and Windproof 26

Will it Rot? 28

Glossary 30

Answers 31

More Books to Read 31

Index 32

Any words appearing in the text in bold, **like this**, are explained in the glossary.

What Is a Natural Material?

Some natural **materials** come from plants or animals. Some natural materials come from the ground. Wood is one kind of natural material. It comes from trees.

This bench is made out of wood.

These things are made of metal or glass.

Metal and glass are natural materials that come from the ground. Metals are found in some rocks. Glass is made from grains of sand that are melted and made into shapes.

5

Some Natural Materials

Some natural **materials** come from plants. Paper comes from wood that has been mashed into **pulp**. Cotton cloth comes from fluffy cotton seeds. Rope may be made from parts of plants.

rope sandals

leather belt

wool sweater

Some natural materials come from animals. Wool for cloth comes from the soft **fleece** of sheep. **Leather** is made from animal skin.

What Is a Man-made Material?

Man-made **materials** are made from **oil**. Most oil lies deep beneath the ground. **Engineers** drill a deep hole to reach the black, runny oil.

Oil is made into many kinds of man-made materials. Plastic is a material made from oil. Is this toy made of a natural material or a man-made material? (Answer on page 31.)

Plastic

Plastic can be made into many different shapes. This factory uses **molds** to make plastic boots. Hot, liquid plastic is poured into each mold. It quickly cools to form the shape of a boot.

safety goggles

Some plastic is very strong. Safety goggles are made of a plastic that is stronger than glass. Plastic can also be very soft. It can be made to feel like skin.

Some Man-made Materials

Some plastic things are **rigid** and cannot bend. Some plastic things are **flexible** and can bend or even be folded over. Which objects in the picture are rigid? (Answer on page 31.)

These things
are made
of plastic.

Plastic can be made to look like a
natural **material**. It can be made to look
like **leather**. Is leather rigid or is it flexible?
(Answer on page 31.)

Glass or Plastic?

These bottles are made of glass. Glass is a natural **material** that is quite strong. But it cracks and breaks easily.

Bottles and drinking glasses can be made of plastic. Plastic is cheaper than glass and does not break as easily when it is dropped. It is also lighter than glass.

China or Plastic?

Plates and cups often are made of china. China is a natural **material**. It is a kind of **clay**, which comes from the ground. It breaks if it is dropped on a hard surface.

Plates and bowls can be made of plastic. Plastic is lighter and cheaper than china. It does not break easily. But it does not feel like china or glass.

Wood, Stone, or Plastic?

Wood comes from trees and **marble** is a hard stone. They are natural **materials**.

wood

marble

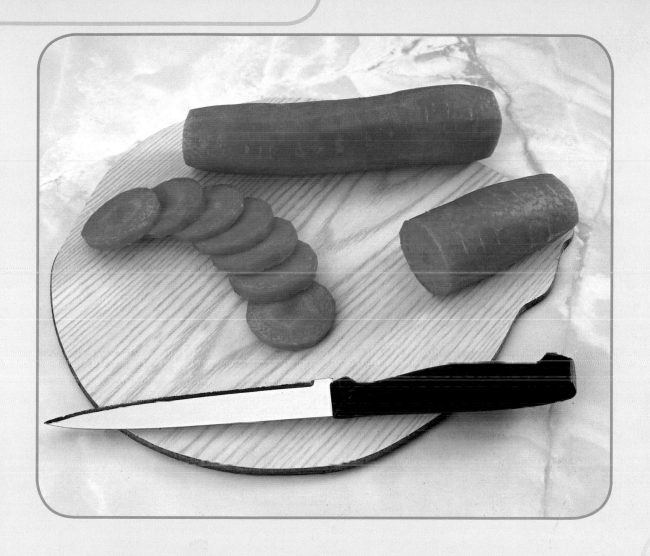

Plastic can be made to look like wood and stone. This chopping board and work surface are covered with thin plastic. The chopping board looks like wood and the work surface looks like marble.

Wax or Plastic?

Candles are made of **wax**. The wax is a man-made **material**. When the candle is lit, the wax melts and soaks into the wick. Plastic cannot do this.

This boy is drawing with colored crayons made of plastic. The girl is drawing with crayons made of wax. The plastic crayons give brighter colors than the wax crayons.

A Mixture of Materials

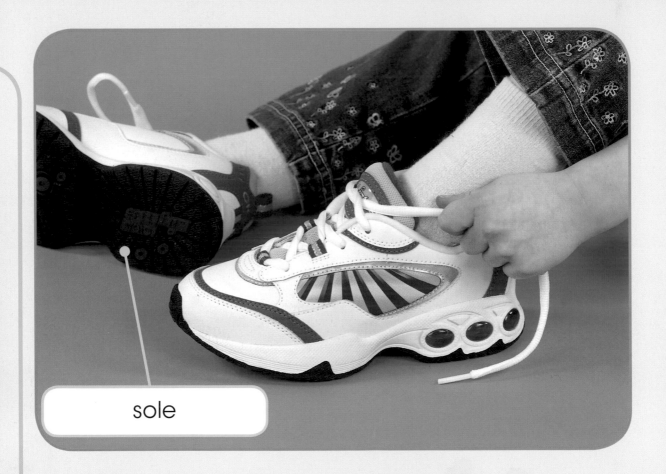

sole

Many things contain natural and man-made **materials**. The top parts of these tennis shoes are made of **leather**. The **soles** are made of man-made material.

The frame of this bicycle is made of
metal. So are the spokes of the wheels.
The seat and the pedals are made of
man-made materials.

Clothes

Many clothes are made of a mixture of natural and man-made **materials**. The materials are mixed together so well that you cannot tell them apart.

This shirt is made of natural materials mixed with man-made materials.

Shirts that contain man-made materials do not crease as much as cotton shirts. This means that they are easier to **iron** smooth.

Warm and Windproof

This girl is wearing a warm **fleece**. It is made of man-made **materials**. It keeps her warm but feels light to wear.

Skiers need to wear clothes that keep out the snow and the wind. These people are wearing special ski pants, coats, and gloves that are made of man-made materials.

Will it Rot?

Things made of wood may **rot** when air and water get into them. Plastic will not rot. But many things made of plastic can be **recycled** to make new things.

Natural **materials** slowly rot and become part of the soil. But garbage dumps are filled with things made of plastic that will never rot away. It is better to recycle these into things that people can use.

Glossary

clay type of heavy soil

engineer someone who builds things like engines, machines, roads, and buildings

fleece fluffy, woolly hair that covers a sheep. A warm, light, and fluffy fabric made of man-made materials is also called fleece.

flexible easy to bend

iron use a hot machine to smooth out the wrinkles in cloth

leather material made from the skin of a cow or other animal

marble smooth, hard stone

material what something is made of

mold hollow shape that is filled with liquid. When the liquid cools, it becomes a solid with the same shape as the mold.

oil a liquid found in the ground. It is used to make gasoline, plastic, and other things.

pulp material that has been squashed and mixed with liquid

recycle change in such a way that it can be used again

rigid not easy to bend

rot slowly break into small pieces

sole the part of the shoe that touches the ground

wax a material that is soft when heated. Most wax is made from oil, but some wax is made by bees.

Answers

Page 9—The toy is made of plastic, which is a man-made material.

Page 12—The mug, sunglasses, and forks and knives are all rigid.

Page 13—Leather is flexible.

More Books to Read

Katz Cooper, Sharon. Exploring Earth's Resources: *Using Water.* Chicago: Raintree, 2007.

Oxlade, Chris. *Rock.* Chicago: Heinemann Library, 2003.

Royston, Angela. *Plastic: Let's look at the Frisbee.* Chicago: Heinemann Library, 2005.

Index

china 16, 17

clay 16

cloth 7

clothes 24, 27

cotton 6

fleece 7, 26

glass 5, 14, 11, 14, 17

ground 4, 5, 8, 16

leather 7, 13, 22

man-made materials 8–9, 12–13, 20, 22, 23, 24, 25, 26, 27

marble 18, 19

metal 5, 23

natural materials 4, 5, 6, 7, 13, 14, 16, 18, 24, 29

oil 8, 9

paper 6

plants 4, 6

plastic 9, 10–13, 15, 17, 19, 20, 21, 28, 29

pulp 6

sand 5

stone 18, 19

wax 20–21

wood 4, 18, 19, 28

wool 7